FROM:

FIRST AID FOR A TEENAGER'S SOUL

Compiled by Marc Anello

Illustrated by Amy Dietrich

PETER PAUPER PRESS, INC
WHITE PLAINS, NEW YORK

Book design by Arlene Greco

Illustrations copyright © 1999
Amy Dietrich

Text copyright © 1999
Peter Pauper Press, Inc.
202 Mamaroneck Avenue
White Plains, NY 10601
ISBN 0-88088-385-5
Printed in China
14   13   12   11   10

Visit us at www.peterpauper.com

FIRST AID FOR A TEENAGER'S SOUL

CONTENTS

INTRODUCTION

Some days are good.
Some days are not so good.

Respect yourself.
Be what you feel. Respect
others—they have much to give.

Define your dreams,
believe in them, and they will
become what is real.

Have fun. Life is now.

BE WHAT YOU FEEL

I [don't] want to be
the next anybody.
I [want] to be the first me!

NATALIE IMBRUGLIA

Don't let anyone tell you that you have to be a certain way. Be unique. Be what you feel.

MELISSA ETHERIDGE

Just be who you are, wait your turn, don't push, be beautiful, be graceful. If you're going to get angry, be angry behind closed doors; don't never let them see you sweat. But just hold your head up, no matter what. Don't let anybody stomp you out.

MARY J. BLIGE

$\mathcal{E}$veryone should start to
become her own role model
in her own image.

EMME

I just don't want to
do anything that doesn't
feel dignified. . . . If you feel
good about what you're doing,
then nothing else matters.

JIM REID

What you believe is what becomes real for you. So if you tell yourself, "I'm disgusting," 50 times a day, then you're brainwashing yourself into believing it, even though it's the furthest thing from the truth.

SABRINA SOLIN

Enjoy who you are.
Don't hate yourself for
what you aren't.

HEATHER GRAHAM

I need to please myself more than I need to please anyone else. If I can't make myself happy, there's no way I'm going to make anyone else happy.

LEANN RIMES

Take the time to gather new
information about yourself.
Maybe some of the stuff you
believe to be true is no longer
valid; perhaps a new you grew
when you weren't looking.

GLAMOUR

What God gave you
was that connection to that
place, but you have to dig for it.
Contacting that place within
you helps you make
the right decisions.

TINA TURNER

Do some self-talk.
Accept yourself and tell
yourself that you're beautiful
inside and out. When you talk
sunshine to yourself, you'll feel
better about yourself.

JANE FLATWATER

[Live] each moment as a new moment, with greater sensitivity to one's thoughts, feelings, and physical sensations. That is the real message of alonetime, and it is through that profound self-awareness, that inner aloneness, that our lives will flower.

ESTER BUCHHOLZ, PH.D.

20

I'm never going to place
myself in a position where
I'm doing something outside
what I want to do, or
what's in my heart.

ICE CUBE

I'm a firm believer that
you can create your own
magic, wherever and
whenever you want.

MICHAEL BOLTON

If you stress out about
a situation . . . your energy,
everything that you put out is
going to come back to you,
so if you put out fun, you're
gonna be fun. If you don't take
everything so seriously, I think
things come easier.

MAIA CAMPBELL

Do something that you respect.
If you can avoid . . . the
celebration of the worthless,
you can't help but augment
your self-respect. And then
you'll probably be happy.

PAUL FUSSELL

The joy of life is made up of obscure and seemingly mundane victories that give us our own small satisfactions.

BILLY JOEL

After a little mental growing and mellowing, the quirky things about the way we look can become our favorites. These days I like being short. It makes me feel sassy when I take on big things and big people. And then, on the days when I need a little help, there are always platform heels.

FRANCESCA DELBANCO

Trust your instincts,
and take control.

JOHN HUSTON

If there were difficult times
when I was growing up,
I got through them by being an
optimist, praying and hoping,
at the risk of sounding clichéd
and corny, that through
music I would rise above
the whole thing . . .

MARIAH CAREY

I believe people should be brave, and I would hate to be subject to my own cowardice.

JEWEL

Holding on to anger only gives
you tense muscles.

JOAN LUNDEN

I've come to learn that
the only real pressure
is the pressure you put
on yourself . . .

PETE SAMPRAS

There is no such thing
as failure. Mistakes happen
in your life to bring into focus
more clearly who you really are.

OPRAH WINFREY

At some point, everyone goes through something difficult in their lives. No one's immune to it. But there are so many other sides to us. . . . we have other things to offer.

ELIZABETH PUNSALAN

I truly believe that the secret to my longevity has been not giving in to the words *no* or *can't* . . .

TYRA BANKS

Confidence and belief in
one's self are almost essential
to success, but conceit is the one
certain poison to kill all chance
of it. Take your victories and
defeats in your stride, and
keep your feet on the ground
and your head a trifle
smaller than your hat.

BILL TILDEN

You have to be yourself.
Be very honest about who
and what you are. And if
people still like you, that's fine.
If they don't, well, that's
their problem.

STING

I think everyone can be cool in their own way if they just let themselves be. If they believe they're cool for themselves and not for other people, then they're cool.

BRENDAN SEXTON III

YOU'RE
NOT IN THIS
BY YOURSELF

You can't expect one friend
to fulfill all your needs.
You have to find different
people and pick who you
talk to about what.

HOPE BOONSHAFT

I find comfort in different people at different times and for different reasons. I'll find comfort in a song. I'll find it in a passage in some book. I'll find it in sharing a laugh with someone.

JAMES VAN DER BEEK

Talking helps alleviate
the sadness. It helps you
understand how you feel
and find a way to resolve
your problems.

RITA GARON,
clinical social worker

There are many complicated issues, but, hey, there are many people of good will. There are some ports in the storm.

BRUCE SPRINGSTEEN

It's kind of great to be
able to really live life, be
with different people
and then realize what's
greatest for you.

KELLY PRESTON

I think that you *are* serving
others when you share
pieces of yourself with
other people.

ANGEL GRANT

[Nelson Mandela] told me
that people should use
their power, whatever it is,
to help others.

NAOMI CAMPBELL

Small acts of heroism done in private are, in a way, more meaningful than visible achievements done in public. You can get glory and applause and awards for things done in public, but you don't for just helping somebody out on a one-to-one level. You just do it for the sake of it, because you want to do it.

JARVIS COCKER

Make God first in your life.
Treat others as you would
want others to treat you.
Have some fun while you're
here. Don't listen to
everything you hear.
And love your mother.

SEAN "PUFFY" COMBS

There is a level of trust
that has to happen. Everyone
has a voice, and I listen.

GOLDIE HAWN

People should talk and relate to each other before they jump into a relationship. You should know each other as friends. I've always felt that.

USHER

I like to make friends with a girl
first. It's all about being real,
getting to know someone—good
sides, bad sides, everything
about each other.

BRANDEN WILLIAMS

A broken heart feels like
the worst thing in the whole
world, but it really helps
you to decide what you
want and don't want.
You learn a lot from
a broken heart.

JENNIFER LOVE HEWITT

Open your eyes.
Listen to the news;
look what's happening
around the world.

SERG TANKIAN

BELIEVE IT— IT BECOMES REAL

Miraculous changes
don't happen overnight.
So take things one
day at a time.

DEDE LAHMAN

Success is never final,
failure is never fatal,
courage always counts.

HIGH SCHOOL WRESTLING MOTTO

The truth is, I've never
run from anything.

JAKOB DYLAN

I have to be allowed room
to do different things. . . .
It's a matter of going forward
and not allowing anybody
to limit you.

JULIA ROBERTS

For me, ambition has become a dirty word. I prefer hunger. To be hungry—great. To have hopes, dreams—great.

JOHNNY DEPP

"Making it," to me, is being the happiest girl in the world. Sometimes I feel that, but it comes out of a sense of peace and friends and love. It is never forced by my career.

ALICIA SILVERSTONE

Life ain't no joke—
you've gotta get into
something positive and
go after what you love to do.

TYRONE BURTON

It's stasis that kills you off in the end, not ambition.

BONO

You have to constantly try
to keep in check why it is
you're doing what you're
doing and not just let inertia
carry you forward.

ETHAN HAWKE

I've never thought, if given the opportunity, I couldn't make good on my goals.

SEAN PATRICK FLANERY

Young people have
an almost biological destiny
to be hopeful.

MARSHALL GANZ

Today, I truly believe
that all people can have hope
if they really want to change.
My own experience has
taught me that anything
is possible.

CHRISTINE LANGLEY

Persistence is the key.
Determination, hard work and
good intentions are all brought
together with persistence. Ignore
the pessimists who want to bring
you down and stand in the way
of your dreams.

JOE MCCULLAUGH

This is just the real world
and I'm growing up.
Life is tough and it's crooked,
but it's pretty fantastic.

BRAD PITT

People talk about things
that are "bigger than life."
There's nothing bigger than life.
Life is big and beautiful as
it is. You just have to take
selections from life and
put it in fiction form. When you
see that, it's just great.

ROBERT DUVALL

Whatever your dream is, whether you want to be an actress or an astronaut or a doctor or a great parent, someone will say you can't do it—and you have to know that you can.

ROSIE O'DONNELL

Don't take life too seriously.
You've gotta take things
for what they are.

LEONARDO DICAPRIO

People who don't want
to weather some of the rough
periods miss out on
something even better.

LISA NIEMI

Just think love.

LAURYN HILL